E♭ ALTO SAXOPHONE
(Baritone Saxophone
E♭ Clarinet, Alto Clarinet)

40 RHYTHMICAL STUDIES

IN UNISON FOR BAND

AF893923

by Grover C. Yaus

BASED ON DIVISION OF MEASURES WITH EASY KEY SIGNATURES

For The Development Of.....

The Individual Player
The Ensemble
The Complete Band

PUBLISHED FOR

PIANO CONDUCTOR
FLUTE
D♭ PICCOLO
B♭ CLARINET
OBOE
E♭ ALTO SAXOPHONE
(Baritone Saxophone
E♭ Clarinet, Alto Clarinet)
B♭ TENOR SAXOPHONE
(Bass Clarinet)
B♭ CORNET
E♭ ALTO (Mellophone)
HORN IN F
TROMBONE (B.C.)
BARITONE (B.C.)
(Bassoon)
BASSES E♭ & BB♭ (Tuba)
DRUMS
BELLS XYLOPHONE-MARIMBA

40 RHYTHMICAL STUDIES

IN UNISON FOR BAND

by Grover C. Yaus

VALUES IN UNISON STUDIES

After a student has mastered division of measure and has become perfect in counting time, even that is not enough, he must develop a style, an accepted style, of handling rhythm, which is gained through experience, and there lies the value of unison material.

An accepted style of handling rhythmic patterns is caught through experience of playing in unison with the best of players, imitating (or stealing) their style of handling rhythm at each rehearsal.

Unison studies are of real value to the busy music instructor, as an advanced student leader can take over a class of mixed instruments and teach them in handling and styling of the different rhythmic patterns, just by playing unison studies with the class.

For warm-up numbers, keep "40 RHYTHMICAL STUDIES" in the band folio throughout the school year, they are of special value to 2nd, 3rd and 4th part players, as they get to play in unison with the solo cornet and get a chance to gain a style of playing that is caught only through experience.

Of great value to a group of students playing different instruments, Example: E♭ Sax, B♭ Clar, Flute, Fr Horn, Trombone and Bass, getting together for a practice session, before school, or after school, or in the home, playing studies in unison, where one will correct the other.

May I also suggest inspection of the Belwin Publications listed below, which are all based on DIVISION of MEASURE, and have become famous as supplementary material for class or individual instruction in the Grade School, High School and College.

"150 Original Exercises"............in unison for Band or Orchestra
"101 Rhythmic Rest Patterns"............in unison for Band or Orchestra
"127 Original Exercises"............in unison for Band or Orchestra
"20 Rhythmical Studies"............in unison for Band Only
"54 Harmonized Rest Patterns"............100% class material, for Band Only
"68 Pares Studies"............in unison for Band or Orchestra

Foreword

These 40 Rhythmical Studies in unison for band are based entirely on division of measure, with easy key signatures.

They are filled with practical rhythms, in a style that makes division of measure interesting.

Each study is written with a kind of rhythmical flow that will help to move the student out beyond the mechanical stage of playing, and will enable him to acquire more of a professional style of handling rhythm.

All lines and measures are identical. Example: 4th measure 3rd line is the same 4th measure 3rd line in all books, including the piano conductor book.

Young Alto and Bass Clarinet players may substitute B♭ Cornet book for Bass Clarinet, and E♭ Mellophone book for Alto Clarinet, if a lower range is required.

To derive the full benefit of these studies, I would suggest working the book through 2 or 3 times, and increase the tempo a little each time.

Eb Alto Saxophone (Eb Baritone Saxophone - Eb Clarinet - Eb Alto Clarinet)

3

March time

4

March time

5

March time

6

Slow March

Slow - strict rhythm

March time

7

March time
f

8

Allegro
f
Slow March
f
March time
f
Waltz lento
p
f
Allegro
f
rit. . . . .

9

10

11

Slow - steady tempo - count 4

12

Slow - short and clean

13

Slow Waltz time

14

March time

15

Steady tempo - count 1

16

Slow March time

17

Slow - steady tempo

18

Slow - strict count

19

March time
f
rit.
Polka time
f
March time
f

20

Slow Drag
f
rit.
Slower
rit.

21

22

23

Slow Waltz - count 3
Strong accent
Grandioso

24

Slow - with clean staccato

25

Slow - even count
f
p
rit.
Very slow - solid staccato
f
3

26

Slow - clean staccato
f
rit.
Much slower

27

Slow- with solid accent

28

Slow with steady count

Very slow

29

Slow - strict count

30

Very slow - strict count - clean-cut style
Slower
rit.

31

32

33

Slow - strict rhythm

34

Slow - solid rhythm

35

Slow - neat staccato style
rit.
Very slow - count 4

36

Slow - with good accent
Strict rhythm
rit.
Much slower

37

Slow - light accent
f
rit.
Slower - neat, clean cut style
p
f

38

Very slow - clean cut style
f
p
rit.
f

39

Very slow - light accent - in 4

40

Very slow - with clean staccato

Alfred